DARK WHEN IT GETS DARK

YVES OLADE

PRAISE FOR KINGDOMS IN THE WILD BOOKS

*

DARK WHEN IT GETS DARK
BY YVES OLADE

Yves Olade is a powerful emerging poetic voice, engaging vehemently with the social unrest and political conditions in postcolonial Nigeria. In this prizewinning chapbook *Dark When it Gets Dark* Olade's multifaceted intricate aesthetics is revealed through the vivid imagery and experimental forms in his poems. —***ATRI MAJUMDER / GOODREADS***

ROOTS GREW WILD
BY ERICA HOFFMEISTER

This book was lovely—a rich and sensuous portrait of a landscape and a family that blossoms from the mundane and wild incidents of everyday life and into the very molecules of soil and animal and earth itself. —***SOPHIE / GOODREADS***

ALL OF US ARE BIRDS & SOME OF US HAVE BROKEN WINGS BY OJO TAIYE

...Taiye also does a beautiful job of blending raw emotion with the technical sophistication of poets like Hanif Abdurraqib and Hieu Minh Nguyen. I was continually awed by his command of language and how he could so clearly evoke precise feelings and moments in time. This book was breathtaking, and if what I've said here interests you, I would recommend giving it a try. —***ELEANOR / GOODREADS***

*

LACE BONE BEASTS: POEMS & FAIRYTALES FOR WICKED GIRLS BY N.L. SHOMPOLE

Holy shit.

Look, I'm seriously picky when it comes to poetry. I've never been super fond of the genre (probably thanks to years spent dissecting it in school) so it takes a lot for me to give a poetry book a high rating. But *Lace Bone Beast* absolutely blew my expectations out of the water. – ***MAGS / NOTGARYCOOPER BOOK REVIEWS***

**THE KINGDOMS IN THE WILD
ANNUAL POETRY PRIZE SERIES**

2020 Dark When it Gets Dark by Yves Olade
2019 All of Us are Birds & Some of Us Have Broken Wings by Ojo Taiye
2018 Roots Grew Wild by Erica Hoffmeister

Published by Kingdoms in the Wild Press LLC
Dark When it Gets Dark Copyright © 2020 Yves Olade
Cover Design: © 2020 Saiteru X.

All Rights Reserved. No part of this publication may be reproduced, stored or transmitted in any form whether written, or electronic without prior written permission from the publisher, except in the case of brief quotations embodied in critical reviews and certain other non-commercial uses as permitted by copyright law. The views and opinions expressed herein are those of the author and do not necessarily reflect the viewpoints, policies, or position of Kingdoms in the Wild Press LLC, its owners, business partners, or employees.

ISBN: 978-1-7331816-2-4
1 2 3 4 5 6 7 8 9 10

Our books may be purchased for libraries, and in bulk for promotional, educational, or business use. Please contact your local librarian or booksellers or Kingdoms in the Wild Press LLC.

WWW.KingdomsintheWild.Com
Follow us on Instagram: @Kingdomsinthewild

CONTENTS

Lagos Winter **1** Lagos Winter II **3** Black Teeth **5** Topograph **7** Savage **8** Trauma Guide to Gunshot Wounds **9** Cut **10** Samarra **11** Panorama of a Dream **12** Incision **13** Désolé **14** Eden **15** Trauma Guide to Gunshot Wounds II **16** Tempest **17** Symptom **18**

Notes **22**

Yves Olade in Conversation **23**

For Nat —
your kindness and generosity
have been such a light.

LAGOS WINTER

In the year of my mother's tongue
& of my father's right hand   see memory
        rain from
heaven like a shower of bullets
        & hear the tear gas sing —   & speak the
language of my fathers fore,
some who lived;   some who died,
        some who swallowed
        ocean like a final meal, blessed
the water over   & over.
            & here there is a gun
        that names my cousins better than I,
      each body like a bullet
lying red in the dirt.
            O wound, O waiting.
      These mourners did not come
to eat   & still leave hungry.
    Wipe that ash from your mouth,
child, scrape the glass   from your throat.
            You know better than to swallow
the gifts   of that vicious sky;
        that fury
                falling on us like rain.

In the year of my brother's shoe,
& my grandfather's dogs,
there is a storm
always on the horizon. See these winds
always incoming tropical & wild.
O madness, O misery. What this
darkness cannot swallow
whole, it must spit out.
What this sun cannot set alight, it
cuts white. See how it
burns & burns & burns
itself out. *Take your own life
in your own hands,
child*. Wet with milk & honey.
Slick with oil and blood. Sing of
black gold red gold. Gold,
in the empty street,
gold, in the desperate night.

LAGOS WINTER II

& in the year of the black stars, of his tight
      fist & his sharp smile: sing *gratitude*
sing   *glory, hallelujah.* O how
      the moon itself does not rise. How
even the crickets pray,   cold hands
      held together,
            begging for one
empty morning.   No caskets: no sons,
      no daughters
            floating in the river.
            Singing hymns
      into the night,
their palms   turned up.   Their bodies
      cold as ice.
Hear the dirt
      cry out   for a night
            with nothing
to grieve,   with no graves to dig
by that gorgeous,   lonely
      roadside.

In the year   of my body
      of my body's own bones
            of my bones' own marrow—

see the sun set the stained glass alight,
    sing *fire come down* to
    brick wall & knife to scythe
& to sword.
        A cut that takes the lover, but
    saves no child. A cut gentle
& perfect as Lagos by moonlight.
    Who stops the mosquito from piercing any
    chest? O wind, O witness. Say
bullet-hole say heart-wound.
        Say, God, *forgive them*
    they know not what they are doing.
    & still, in the night,
hear us sing into the darkness
        & dance into the
    hunger of the earth
    this wild & jealous earth
    we call
        our country.

BLACK TEETH

black teeth in the
white night. you
tidy. you total. *who
could love you
now?* this stillness.
this grief. O, un-
quiet body. dis-
quiet soul. O hands
of milk & honey.
cleaved clean at the
bone. say wrist to
wrist. say body to
perfect body. *who
could call you lovely
now?* you weak,
you tender. *Where is
the knife for your
hand?* nails blunt
with grief. stomach
empty of desire. why
not devour all that
you are given? all
that you have not
been given? between

a predator and its
prey there is only
hunger, and desire
has no direction. *a
lamb that will not bite
the wolf was not
born hungry enough.*
but I was born hungry
enough. I am not
afraid of anything.
you kind, you breaking.
sing of all these
shepherds' sons and
the slings in their hands,
slick as the oil on their
tongues. O wine, O water.
I am not afraid of anyone;
even the boy with the
mark on his head
to tell me of the rock
in his hand.

TOPOGRAPH

This night I have   no longing, left. call me haunting,   call me chaos.   say   disaster   & disaster   & disaster.   streets red as gold   with blood. child, I   need no pity,   I spilled it   all myself yes, I   broke &   broke & broke again.   *O God, what do I do   with   all my   hungry?   all my empty?*
What if He   has nothing to say?   call this house   of forgiveness.   call this river of   grief. teeth   blunt   to the gum,   tongue   bloodstained   tongue bleeding.   I   will take   even that   which does   not belong to me.   I take apart   & put together. build &   break &   break.   How I am not afraid   of anything.   No darkness   & no longing
           but the shadow of my body   and its distance   from me.

SAVAGE

Mother, see me bow over the toilet? spit up
stormclouds? spill my blood for the drain?
say, *dirty hands* and *dirty waters. who could
call you gentle now?* body like a wreckage by the
side of the road? say carrion, say kindness. perhaps
this too is violence. & so is absence & so is empti-
ness. staircase rising red, but no entrance, no
exit. *who but God will love you like this?* hungry
as the riverbed, hungry as the feast? there is a
story in that, somewhere. pulling up the carpets to
strip the room bare. it's in the music. it's the mourning.
salt in the wound. cuts on the scar-line. how it's
August before it's over. dancing in the garden, wild
with memory. how a man touches another man
before the dream begins. *yes, but the dream—
how always it ends.* between summer and winter,
that space becoming endless. that longing unmooring
your body. you angry,   you vicious & free.
throwing stones into the river. casting open your sins.
letting what has been taken, be taken. again & again
& again. *who could call you gentle now? you cruel, you
savage thing?*

TRAUMA GUIDE TO GUNSHOT WOUNDS

in the end I · took it all · my mouth undone · my head tipped back · your thumb · blooming bruise · waxing trauma · on my jaw · see me open · so wide · to take communion · and take it well · how I · don't even · taste · the blood · just felt the burn · going down · and how · it didn't · mean a thing · it didn't matter · at all · only proved that · like a bullet · confession can't · be held · under the tongue · only fired · from the throat · into any body · kind enough · to take it whole · absolution · in exchange · for doing · unto others · what they · have done · unto you · but violence · is built · to be wider · always · on the other side · sing elegies · to the exit wound · but pain · is still · the shortest distance · between · two bodies · is still · the only ghost · between the human · and divine · and in · trying · to haunt the distance · I turned · the chamber · of a gun · and dared to ask · for its truth · there is nothing · but death · on the other side · singing its own · hymns · praying its own · prayers · I learnt · that liturgy's lesson · throwing myself · from buildings · to wonder · at what · I could survive · if given the opportunity · but every martyr · knows · that at the end · of every draw · is · another barrel · to look down · to beg God · to be delivered from · the heart beating · itself bruised · heart beating · out apology · after apology · the blood · becoming · its own · sacrament · the body broken · into pieces · small · enough to · consume and · not enough · to satisfy.

CUT

Now you need his love again, like it's summer, and there's blood by the river-bank. Call it longing. Call it lovely. Perfect as the shot bird. Calm as oil on water. You could bleed until the river remembers where it is going. First, it was Autumn. Now, somehow, it's over. You, in the kitchen. You, on the floor. Peaches cut in gentle pieces. Peaches sweet as his desire. *How hungry are you now?* Windows cracked open. White laundry outside. Here, listen to birds remember how to be birds. Listen to the song of becoming what you forgot you were. You are not the god of this memory. *Summer to winter*, and back again. This, you've heard before. Ravens on the washing line. Night falling open. How it was dusk and dawn and dusk again. *Dusk and dawn and dusk*. Yes, the river. The music and the dancing. Yes, and the birds — their sweet wings broken. The moon and its white hunt. You, unbecoming. Like his mouth has made you with the sweetest violence, his hands the most holy ruin. *You could pull the stars apart and still be gentle in the morning.* You who never touched anything without wanting to destroy it. You who never loved anything at all. See your body in the river float. Your body in the river sinking. Your body in the river slit from hip to thigh, from knee to neck and collarbone.

SAMARRA

yes, I wanted to be everything
    & in love as well. felt the shock of
        each fall like a gentling. *O*
            hunger after hunger. grief
chasing grief. his hands on my
    jaw. his body on my body. blue
        eyes and a white smile. Blue
            eyes and a strong back-
hand. how stupid I was. how
    lonely. clawing desperate at
        the dirt. O desert. O coyote.
            empty as that hollow earth,
tragedy haunting tragedy.
    crawling like a child towards
        any exit. suffering so well,
            I could do it in my sleep.
say love like a summer
    morning. say anger like a
        gut-wound. twist the knife
            a little deeper, darling.
heart like a river-mouth.
    all I am & all I was: foolish
        enough to have come back;
            foolish enough to have gone.

PANORAMA OF A DREAM

This, the darkness. This, the danger. Story of disaster. Story of grief. Always waking from the same dream. Buried to my wrists in the dirt. Dust to dust. Ashes to ashes. I didn't know it would feel like this. Always opening and closing. Building & breaking. Coming home so I could always be leaving. This, the sidewalk. This, the door. Here I walk and keep walking. So far I cast a shadow, long over it all. How far is anything from anything else? This, the absence. This, the distance. From body through to body. From grief to new grief. The sun in August. The sun in autumn. Heart of despair, burning on the porch. House at midnight, house at dawn. Staircase red with fear. Staircase blue with longing. Say killing, say kindness. From room to room, from morning through to morning

INCISION

& we're in love, so how I suffer. I suffer only
for him. One hand on my neck. One hand

on my wrist. A garland of bruising as he tries
to kiss my mouth wider. to bite my lips bloody.

& After all this time, I've somehow learned
nothing. I say, *If you love me, make a corpse of*

me. Make an autopsy. Begging touch like a steel
trap. All lockjaw. All broken hinge. For me, it's

always hunting season. June, July, August.
Summer always cut so perfectly. Here, I try to

close the wounds I make. I try and break that
distance. Hand on my neck. Fist by my eye. Up to

his wrists in the center of me, pulling it all apart.
This love that takes us from bloodsport to slaughter-

house— I've had nightmares end more
gently than that.

DÉSOLÉ

something about the wound & the blood by
the pool. all summer wide & all summer long. how
he'd hunt you to extinction if he could. say shatter,
say splint. mourning sweet on your lips. the killing
kindness of some wretched thing. how you'd cut
yourself open on his longing. how easy it was to
desire your grief. O milk, O honey. O perfect &
perfection. cut from wrist to wrist, bleeding over
everything. *what creature are you becoming?*
clawing your skin to ribbons? eating your own
hunger? begging your blood back into his hands?
body in the river, body in the lake. body in the
water tells you autumn is over. *say winter, say fall.*
gentle as his hands around your throat. perfect as
the red fruit, bruising   between itself and the floor.

EDEN

Andrew won't you love me in summer, love
me in that warm   winter rain? Hold my
head underwater, so sweet. Like you mean it,
like you always meant to save me. Call it
morning, call it mourning. Perfect as the slain
faun. How we broke the skin of the water &
called it holy. How holy it was. The awesome
quiet of the space between a lover and his God.
Gorgeous this side of death. Perfect this side of
the river. Not enough to make you clean, but
enough to wash the blood off. Eat the peach &
spit the stone out. Your taste a razor on my tongue.
Making good mistakes with those hopeless hands.
One after another & another &

TRAUMA GUIDE TO GUNSHOT WOUNDS II

mother said · I could be anything · I wanted · the space · between atoms · the rain · on the street · corner · *and God* · I prayed · *Father* · make me · both the bullet · and the finger · on the trigger · the distance · and distance vanishing · in every breath · veins held · together · by fingertips · and faith · holding apart · what should · come together · making home · what is holy · and holy again · yes, · to let the lead · tear clean · through your skin · is to remember · how much more · it hurts · to let go · than it does · to hold on · to any killer · kind enough · to let you catch it · slow · crucify · yourself gentle · to be your own · merciful · executioner · like this · you can have anything you want · believe in any myth · including · yourself · believe that any weapon · can be other · than what it is · do other · than for what it was made · yes, and · isn't that love · after all? · is it not · worth · dying for? · one chance · to press · the gun · to your body · to beg the body · not to leave · you · again · but ask · the right saint · and he'll speak · of how death · always comes · more than · once · how every · wound · mirrors regret · is both itself · and its reflection · like an arrow · buried holy · to the hilt · it doesn't matter · what kills you · just that something · does · how you go · so sweet · to your knees · for violence · and violence · alone · each body · sings its own · song · sings agony · sings grief · a memory · a promise · that what · cruelty · puts in · to you · it will somehow · take out · again.

TEMPEST

& you were standing in the doorway   casting judgement
like a child casts his stones into the lake   singing,
who shall wear the robe, Lord? who shall wear the crown?
rising &   rising,   biblical in flood
hungry as the whale who   opened her mouth &
made a feast   of devot-   ion   who swallowed &
made perfect the swallowing   & O sin, O safety   pouring
oil into the basin   salting white the sea   God,   I've
never had my heart broken   by a beautiful thing.   Now,
who could call me   unclean?
All hollowed out   pristine.   So empty   so
empty &   rising, & rising   like a Lazarus   like
the flood   -gate   Baptized new &   praying to
become something else.   Even dead.   Even
lonely.   Chaos moving dark over those black waters.
The shadow of a dream in the light say, *hungry ghost*   say
holy ghost   say *break*
& break   &   be loved new,   in the breaking. O
time, O tempest,
O beginning and ending.

SYMPTOM

after Reyna N. A

The remedy for pain is always more pain.
There's a logic in that. The way
the radio plays that old song to remind you of autumn.
It takes you back. How memory makes everything worse.
That August. Everything red and still on fire,
and what you held came apart in your hands.
The rest of the story still catches in your mouth.
How it's always too soon. How you never open up.
Time has its own axis, turning out of joint.
Things come around on their own.
Or they don't. And nothing lasts forever,
after all. Which is true.
But it matters. Or it doesn't. See,
you've forgotten where the river is going.
You've forgotten what the story is for.   But the body
was at the crux of things, fixed at the center.
All that balance. Those sharp corners.
That bullet turning over in your mind.
Killing becoming kindness the longer you watch.
Say it was Cain who pulled the trigger,
creating a new cruelty.
Speaking something awful into the world.
Inventing one more terrible
thing for a person to do to another.
God marked him up to remind him.

Abel was the one who wanted to forget.
And who can blame him? Dying to get away from it all?
Who could want a brother like that?
Like this, you fold sorrow in on itself, until
it's too small to do you any damage.
It's beautiful: how there are so many
things you can do with your hands.
You could even put the stone down.
Clap twice and the lights go dark. Now,
the radio plays another song.
Dancing in the porchlight. Kicking up splinters.
How the night always steals the silence from your throat.
Now your lips are moving, you can't make them stop.
You don't know what to do with your mouth when it's empty.
       But really, you just have to talk.
Isn't this what the story was for?
Something always leaks out anyway,
no matter how you cut your tongue up.
Why are you holding all that blood in your mouth
instead of swallowing it down?
Or better yet, spitting it out. If you have
something to say, *spit it out*.
You, like a deer, caught in headlights.
There's nothing left but the road bending right.
And both of us, in the middle, becoming accidents
of ourselves.

Here we are driving in circles. Hitting parked cars.
Getting lost in open fields, watching the birds remember
they used to be birds. Where do we go from here?
Which way is north? It matters. Or somehow, it doesn't.
Say something true and mean it.
Watch the world tilt on its axis.
This is what the story is for.
A lie is just a memory told in the wrong order.
You'll get there eventually. After all,
there's nowhere else to go.
You can move things around, but the things are still there.
Where else are you going to put them?
It's hard to tell in the dark.
Feel your way around the problem. Make good
use of those hands, that tongue.
The sides of this story seem infinite. Really, there's only one.
Look at you, you're a librarian. A historian.
You're putting all those words back where they belong.
It's ingenious. A miracle.
You haven't learnt anything at all.
See, you have to let go before
things can land the right way up.
But you're always trying so hard to hold on.
Look, there are only two sides to touch.
Somehow, you're always on the wrong one.
Is this what it means to talk about love?

Look at that heart of yours, breaking into pieces.
Setting up to fall.
See it make violence the center of things.
How it doesn't know where to go.
You think the remedy for pain is always more pain.
This too, I think, is a symptom

NOTES

1. *Trauma Guide to Gunshot Wounds* was previously published in *The Anatomy of Desire—The Poetry Annals* 2018.

2. *Trauma Guide to Gunshot Wounds II* was previously published in *The Ellis Review* 2018.

3. *Symptom (after Reyna N. A.)* was previously published in *The Anatomy of Desire—The Poetry Annals* 2018.

YVES OLADE
IN CONVERSATION

Let's get right to it, what inspired *Dark When it Gets Dark*?

I usually have a lot of trouble coming up with names and titles, both for individual poems and collections, so *Dark When it Gets Dark* is exciting to me because it's one of the only times I've started with a title, then built a body of work around it. The line came originally from a poem (since edited out) which read in full, "I pray one day / it will be dark / when it gets / dark." It means a lot of things to me, but I think primarily I wanted to talk about honesty and write about the power of something being wholly and fully itself, regardless of whether it is "good" or "bad."

Were you trying to tackle a particular subject, theme, or topic in your chapbook Dark When It Gets Dark?

To return to the idea of honesty, I think I really wanted to explore that more, in a world where the grounds of perception itself seem to be constantly shifting beneath our feet. What a blessing it would be to look at something and know that you see all of it: no deception, no concealment—just darkness when it's dark. I'm not sure how consistently this comes through as a theme, but it was definitely something very prominent in my mind while I was writing.

You are an ancient history graduate, and your love for history is apparent in your work. Do you try to integrate history into your writing, or does it come naturally? What does the process of integrating your studies in your creative writing look like?

My degree is definitely an ongoing point of reference for me. In some ways, it's such a large part of my life that it seems natural and inevitable that it would find its way into my work. On the other hand, this blurring of boundaries is sometimes a very deliberate process. Poetry becomes a way for me to explore my research themes in a more free and open way, and my research sometimes provides the inspiration and impetus to write. The lines between the two are not very well defined, but there's definitely a symbiotic relationship between them.

What is an obscure thing you find interesting about the world?

Something I've recently become interested in is naming practices across time and throughout history. I've always been aware that the way I came by my name (as a person with Yoruba parents) was different from how my English friends were named, but I honestly never gave it much thought. However, I recently found out that there are millions of ancient Greek names on record, and recurrences in names are incredibly rare. Isn't that astonishing? A language community that large and no one has the same name? I find that so wonderful and so interesting.

What does your writing process look like?

It's messy! I go long periods without writing a word, and then I'll sit down and write five poems at once. I'll put a note on my phone when I think of a line I like, but I won't write the rest of the poem for maybe another year. I'll get out of bed at two in the morning because there's something I just *have* to write down, or I'll sit in front of my open laptop for weeks on end, fiddling with the wording of one verse. It's messy, but I've learned to lean into that messiness and appreciate my capacity to create in whatever form it decides to manifest. I'm not interested in forcing it anymore.

This has been a shocking year for all of us, has the COVID-19 pandemic affected your ability to create? How so?

On the one hand, like many others, the pandemic shook up my schedule and made me rethink how I was spending my time. I lost my two-hour commute, I lived with my parents again, and I wasn't allowed to leave the house. So while I definitely had more time to create (and made use of that time!), I also was grappling more widely with thinking about how to use my one wild & precious life (Mary Oliver).

Has COVID-19 changed how you view and/or navigate the world? How so?

I think I'm just continually amazed by people. I think it's especially at times of crisis that we start to see with ever-increasing clarity the real extremes of human nature. Not only people at their most callous and cruel, but also people at their kindest and most connected. I'm trying my hardest to lean into that connection. So when an elderly lady at the pharmacy asks me to help her carry her bag up the escalator, I can think, "this can still happen anywhere / not everything is lost" (Naomi Shihab Nye) and believe it.

What has been the most startling thing you've learned or experienced since the pandemic began?

I've definitely learned a lot about myself over the past few months. Honestly, a lot of it hasn't impressed me, but my capacity for growth has really amazed me. It perhaps sounds arrogant to talk about myself as a "startling thing" to learn about or experience, but I've spent most of my life believing that I'm not built to function in the world—not really. For the most part, I still believe that. But I also have to say that it's been such a pleasure and joy to discover and start to believe in my own internal abundance over the past year.

You are one of the first poets we published on Kingdoms in the Wild almost four years ago. How has your poetry or writing process changed since then?

I definitely think I'm more relaxed than I was a few years ago. Some of the people who read my poetry like the new me less, I think, but that's okay. I don't think being so intense all the time was good for me, and honestly, I think that came out in my poetry. I definitely see poetry less like a platform I was trying to climb onto or a house I was trying to break into. Now, poetry is like an old friend I often invite for dinner, but who I bear no grudge against if they decide not to come.

Are there any themes or reoccurring threads that you try to explore in your writing? How have these changed over the years?

I talk about blood a lot. Blood and love, the color red, the color blue. Longing and desire. Human bodies and bodies of water. Birds and bones, anger and kindness, cruelty, and beauty. Honestly, I tend to conceptualize my work less as a series of poems and more as the same poem, written over and over again in different ways. It used to worry me, and I thought that people would get bored of me talking about lakes and lovers all the time, but it hasn't happened yet!

Where do you see yourself and/or your work this time next year, any big goals or projects on your mind?

Well, I'm hoping that poetry still comes to dinner every so often. Other than that, I'm just really open to trying new things. I'd love to do a zine or an experimental poetry chapbook—something that combines art and words to make something exciting. There's definitely no rush with that, and if it happens next year, it happens. If not, I'm willing to wait for it. I guess I don't believe in forcing it anymore.

What other art form influences or informs your writing?

I love all forms of art. I listen to a lot of music, I have a collage of paintings on my wall, and I draw and doodle whenever I get the chance. Art is just such a powerful and beautiful way of experiencing the world and being open to those experiences. I love the way a song can change your mood or how a film can break your heart. It might be a stretch to draw any concrete connecting lines, but these things definitely inform my own artistic processes and how I try and construct experiences through a poem or a piece.

What has been the hardest part of this year regarding your creative work?

I don't imagine that I'm unique in this, but it just felt like there hasn't been enough time or that, when there was time, I should be doing something else—something more "important". It's taking some work to accept that the things that make me happy *are* important and that they deserve my time and attention. The amount of suffering in the world necessitates rather than precludes the creation of joy.

What do you think the post-pandemic world will look like 5 years from now? 10 years from now?

I have no idea! I can't even pretend to know. I have hopes, of course, but I think that if the pandemic has taught me anything, it's that our imagined futures are fragile things. I'm planning only very gently now and staying open to the world as it transfigures and re-figures itself. Additionally, I think that whatever it is we want to see in five or ten years, we have to start building it now. If you want flowers to grow, it's a good idea to plant flowers.

What has been the most rewarding part of this year?

I think my scholarship was definitely a moment of extreme catharsis and relief: that all the work I had done had paid off in a meaningful way. It was so important to me not just as a "moment" this year, but as the culmination of several years, and it meant that I could go back to doing something I really loved (being a historian!), so I really couldn't have asked for more.

What's an underrated (or little recognized) book you love?

I love *Eromenos* by Melanie McDonald. The story of Hadrian and Antinous from Antinous' perspective. It's absolutely devastating, and I couldn't recommend it highly enough.

What's your favorite way to unplug?

I love doing nothing. This sounds ridiculous, but honestly, lying in bed or on my floor, flicking mindlessly through the same six apps on my phone is so relaxing for me and is one of the only times I feel like I'm truly taking time "off." I also love taking naps and tend to have at least one a day.

Where can readers find you?

I'm on Tumblr still at yvesolade.tumblr.com, on Twitter at @yvesolade, and (peripherally) on Instagram @yvesolade – I mainly only use Instagram to watch my friends' stories, film walks I go on, and upload videos of myself making elaborate coffee drinks, but I'm happy to be found there all the same!

*

ABOUT THE AUTHOR

Yves Olade is an ancient history graduate and insomniac who lives on the south coast of England. He's been featured *in Kingdoms in the Wild, Glass, The Ellis Review,* and the *Rising Phoenix Review*. He recently became a runner up in the *What Are Birds?* Transpoetics prize. An avid documentary fan, he loves mobile games, evenings & lemonade. He self-published two chapbooks called *Bloodsport* (2017) and *Slaughterhouse* (2020).

More from Yves Olade:

Twitter: @yvesolade
Website: www.yvesolade.tumblr.com

LIKED THIS BOOK?
PLEASE CONSIDER LEAVING A REVIEW

Reviews are extremely important for books and are particularly crucial for small independent publishers like Kingdoms in the Wild Press. Word of mouth and your reviews help people find our books and drive sales, which gives us the chance to acquire and publish more books such as this chapbook and our poetry pamphlets.

Where to leave reviews:
Goodreads & Amazon
Book Review Blogs and Websites
Podcasts or Library Websites
Independent Bookstores Websites

You can also tell others about this book & Kingdoms in the Wild on your social media networks.

Where to find us:

Website: KingdomsintheWild.Com
Instagram: @kingdomsinthewild

Your support is forever appreciated.

Kindly,
Kingdoms in the Wild Team

MORE FROM KINGDOMS IN THE WILD

House of Unholy Dreams by Adira Bennett
This is How the Light Gets In by Hinnah Mian
Red Chapel by Catherine Hou
Roots Grew Wild by Erica Hoffmeister

COPYRIGHTS

Dark When It Gets Dark
Copyright © 2020 Yves Olade
All Rights Reserved

Cover Design © Saiteru X.
Cover and Interior Design
© 2020 Kingdoms in the Wild Press LLC
Original Cover Image Courtesy of
Unsplash.Com–Andrew Russian

Dark When It Gets Dark was published by
Kingdoms in the Wild Press LLC
Edited by L. Naisula
www.KingdomsintheWild.com
All Rights Reserved

KINGDOMS IN THE WILD PRESS LLC
974 P.O. Box
Pullman, WA
99163

PRINT
ISBN: 978-1-7331816-2-4

DIGITAL
ASIN: B08NB6XS8G

First Edition: December 2020
1 2 3 4 5 6 7 8 9 10

KINGDOMS IN THE WILD PRESS

Is the place for original, experimental, and cutting-edge poetry and fiction. We strive to bring you work that reflects the world's complex and intertwined cultures and histories. Join the conversation by visiting our site today [KINGDOMSINTHEWILD. COM](http://KINGDOMSINTHEWILD.COM)

Printed in Great Britain
by Amazon